Lisa Marino and Lynn Peters

Spumoni & Friends

We Can Ride the Bus!

Story by Lisa Marino
Photographs (unless otherwise noted) by Lynn Peters

Acknowledgement

Special Thanks to: bus driver, Bobbie V. Allen for getting permission to use her bus for the photos and Frederick Co. Schools Transportation and Shenandoah Valley Westminster – Canterbury assisted living for use of the buses in Winchester, VA.

WOW!

It's the first day of school! Time to ride the bus! Boy, are we excited!

Wait on the side of the road.

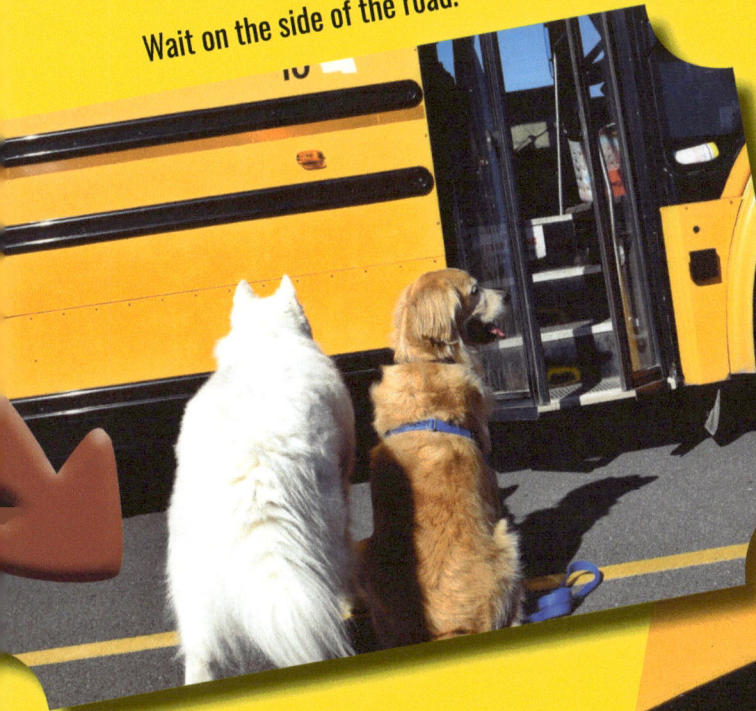

STAY SAFE!

Wait quietly behind the line.

We can't wait to ride. But see where we sit? We're behind the line, where it's safe.

5

We wait until it's the right time to get on the bus.

Smart, Spumoni! He knows how to wait patiently.

When the door opens, get on the bus slowly.

The door opens. We get more and more excited. But we go carefully up the stairs, like Spumoni does!

See what we hold?
It's the handrail.

Holding the
handrail helps
make sure we
don't fall.

Good work,
Spumoni!

Hold the handrail!

8

Sometimes the bus engine is really really loud. It can feel a little scary! But Tucker and Skipper know it's ok. That's just how buses sound.

Find a seat quickly. Sit facing forward.

Okay, it's time to find a seat. We have to do this quickly because we don't want to make the bus late! We all want to get to school on time.

Do NOT stand on the bus seat!

Sitting is a better choice.

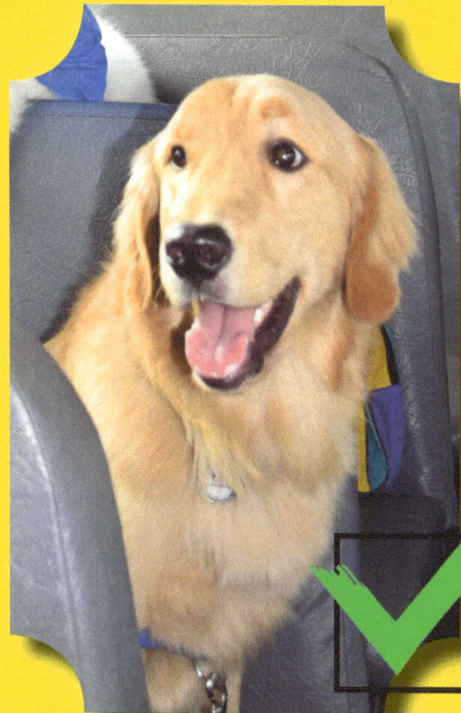

Sometimes we get so excited, we just want to stand up. Or we want to hang over the seat in front of us. But that's not safe. We could fall if the bus moves or stops suddenly. Sitting is the better choice. Sit, Spumoni! Sit!

No, no, Spumoni! Don't kneel on the seat! And don't turn around to talk. It's better to sit and speak quietly to whomever is next to you. That's practicing safety and good manners, too.

Do NOT talk to the person behind you!

Talking quietly to the person next to you is a better choice.

Do NOT yell out the bus window!
Looking out the window quietly is a better choice.

Spumoni! Yelling out the bus window and putting our paws out is not the right thing to do! But we can sit and look out the window. There's lots to see as we drive along the route to school.

Keep all hands and objects inside the bus!

Good job, Spumoni! Bring those paws back in. And keep all your belongings on the seat or on the floor, not near the window where they could fall out. You wouldn't want to lose your backpack!

When you arrive at school, wait for the driver's permission to get up.

Hurray! We've arrived! Look how good we're all sitting! Now we will wait for the bus driver to tell us when to get up to leave the bus.

Thank the driver. It's polite to do!

We say thank you to the driver. It's the polite thing to do. Wait. Spumoni! You're not the driver! Get down from there. Be good like Biscotti, Zamboni and Skipper.

We make sure we take all our things with us. And we throw our trash away. Nice job, Spumoni! You're doing the right thing, now!

Take all of your belongings. Pick up your trash.

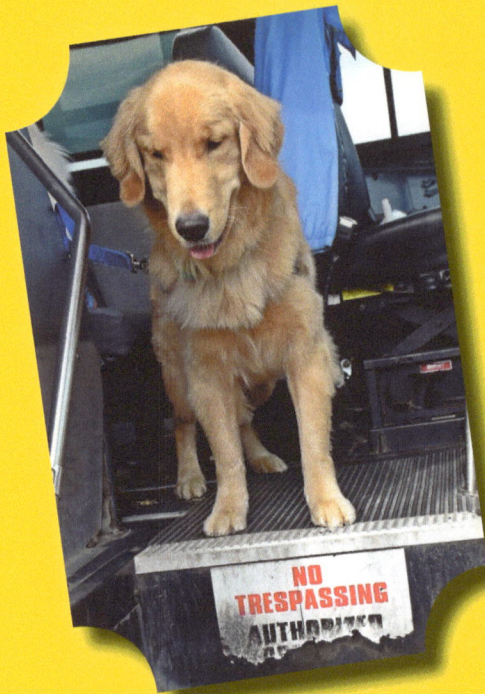

Exit slowly. Watch your step.

This is so exciting! But we're always careful. We exit slowly and watch our step.

Skipper is really good at waiting his turn. Way to go, Skipper!

Sometimes one of us will have to use a wheelchair lift. This isn't a toy, and we only use it when we need to. We sit still when we're on the chair lift. We don't want to fall. Good job, Zamboni!

If you use the chair lift, sit still while riding up or down.

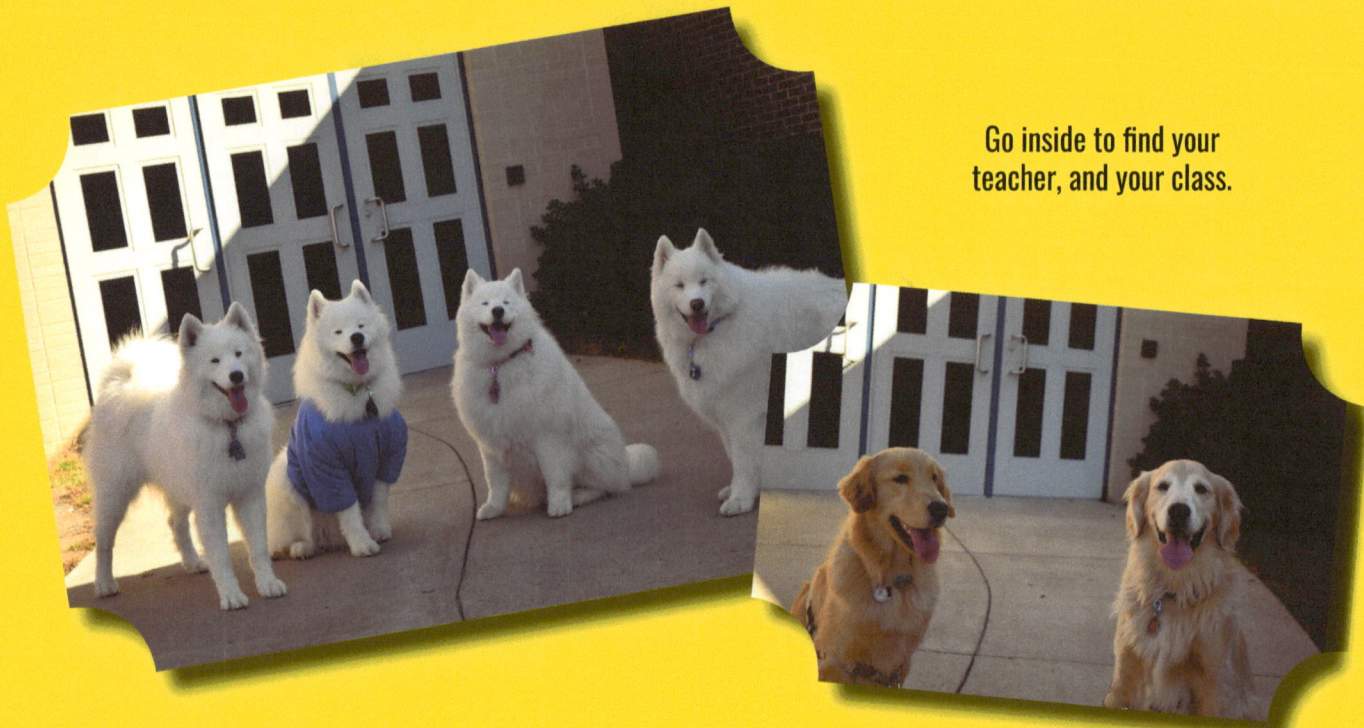

Go inside to find your teacher, and your class.

It's time to go inside the school now.

We can't wait to meet our teachers!

The End.

Goodbye, bus! We'll see you when you come back at the end of the school day.

Spumoni

Spumoni is a 6 year old Samoyed who LOVES kids, and puts on trick shows at libraries and schools. He loves learning new things and is a little bit naughty! He likes to make people laugh, and is a Comfort Dog helping people affected by crises.

Biscotti

Biscotti is a 4 year old Samoyed who likes to visit people in nursing homes. She does tricks and likes to learn. She likes to be outdoors in nature and pull scooters, hike, do Agility and chase bunnies.

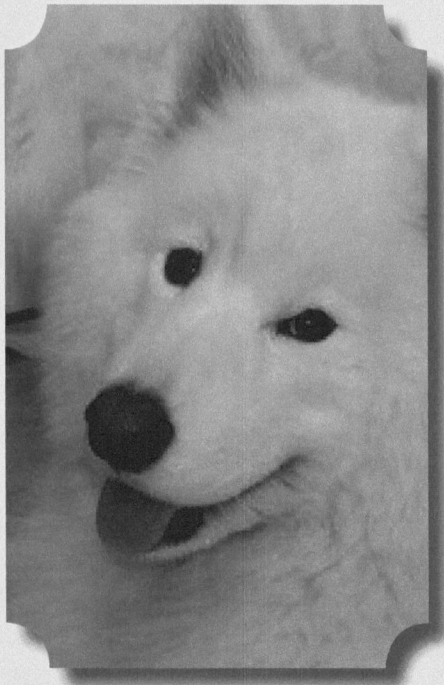

Zamboni

Zamboni is a 9 year old Samoyed who likes to visit with kids, and listen to books. She plays sports like Agility, and herding sheep, and chasing bunnies. She is a Comfort Dog who helps people affected by crises.

Gelato

Gelato is an 11 year old Samoyed who loves to do reading visits with kids and listen to books! He brings cheer to people in nursing homes, and is a Comfort Dog for people affected by crises. He loves helping people.

Skipper

Skipper is a 3 year old Golden Retriever who loves visiting children in schools and also residents in nursing homes.

Tucker

Tucker is a 5 year old Golden Retriever. He loves to visit children in schools, and also residents in nursing homes.

www.ingramcontent.com/pod-product-compliance
Lightning Source LLC
Chambersburg PA
CBHW041558040426

42447CB00002B/217